99 Ways
to Fight Worry
and Stress

D0107144

99 Ways to Fight Worry and Stress

Elsa Kok Colopy

WATERBROOK
PRESS

99 WAYS TO FIGHT WORRY AND STRESS
PUBLISHED BY WATERBROOK PRESS
12265 Oracle Boulevard, Suite 200
Colorado Springs, Colorado 80921

Details in some anecdotes and stories have been changed to protect the identities of the persons involved.

ISBN 978-0-307-45837-7
ISBN 978-0-307-45843-8 (electronic)

Published in the United States by WaterBrook Multnomah, an imprint of the Crown Publishing Group, a division of Random House Inc., New York.

WATERBROOK and its deer colophon are registered trademarks of Random House Inc.

Library of Congress Cataloging-in-Publication Data
Colopy, Elsa Kok.
    99 ways to fight worry and stress / Elsa Kok Colopy.—1st ed.
      p. cm.
    ISBN 978-0-307-45837-7— ISBN 978-0-307-45843-8 (electronic)
1. Worry—Religious aspects—Christianity. 2. Stress management—Religious aspects—Christianity. I. Title. II. Title: Ninety-nine ways to fight worry and stress.
    BV4908.5.C65 2009
    155.9'042—dc22

                                            2009011068

Printed in the United States of America
2009—First Edition

10 9 8 7 6 5 4 3 2 1

SPECIAL SALES
Most WaterBrook Multnomah books are available at special quantity discounts when purchased in bulk by corporations, organizations, and special-interest groups. Custom imprinting or excerpting can also be done to fit special needs. For information, please e-mail SpecialMarkets@WaterBrookMultnomah.com or call 1-800-603-7051.

Contents

Introduction

I wish I could say I handle stress and worry with ease. Two
years ago I would have told you that I could handle most
anything thrown my way. I'm strong. I work out. I eat oatmeal and pray nearly every day. What more does one need
to face the hard times?

Then life came. I had a kidney go bad and required nine
hours of surgery to get back on track. A few months later, I
was in a bad car wreck. Then my husband lost his job, my
daughter's appendix ruptured, and we moved across the
country. Then there was the small stress of trying to sell a
house in a pitiful economy, even as we moved into a two-
bedroom apartment with what I'm certain was a rock band
(and their roadies) living above us. Then just to keep things
interesting, our adult son moved back in with us and is, as
I write these words, in need of a kidney transplant. My husband will be the donor. I don't feel so invincible anymore.

I need more than oatmeal and exercise. I need tools. I

need day-to-day coping-with-life tools so I don't follow through on my temptation to move to the mountains with twenty pounds of chocolate, a few warm blankets, and an armload of romantic comedies.

I figure you understand my pain. You wouldn't have picked up this book if you didn't have your own litany of life stuff—things you never expected to happen—worries, fears, heartbreak, stress over finances, marriages, kids, illness.

So join me. Join me as I investigate healthy ways to handle the worry and productive ways to walk through the stress. And maybe together we can move forward, not into our hiding places of choice, but through this season into hope, with smiles on our faces.

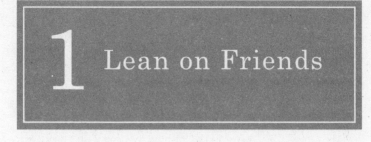

1 Lean on Friends

A friend loves at all times.
—PROVERBS 17:17

I prefer to keep my worries private. It's my pride that gets in the way. It feels more comfortable to be little known and viewed as strong than to be exposed. And yet I face a difficult season ahead. Health concerns are at the forefront. Financial strain weighs heavy. Other worrisome circumstances litter the horizon, and I have come to one conclusion: I cannot do this alone. It will be tough to call a friend when I'm stressed, but I'll do it. I don't want to run to unhealthy hiding places, so I need the strong shoulders of safe friends more than ever.

You may identify. If so, read on. Here are some practical ways to build friendship and then lean on those you come to trust.

1 SCHEDULE TIME

If I don't set up a time to connect with my friends, it simply won't happen. The passing "Let's do lunch" usually means "Let's not do lunch, we're both too busy."

So I've learned a better way. My friend Jennifer is one of the strong shoulders I lean on. We have to set a weekly time to talk. Sure, we've fallen off the wagon and gone weeks without connecting, but we rearrange life to make it work. We've actually determined that the best way to stay in each other's worlds is to talk at 5:30 a.m. on Thursday mornings. My friend Lauriza meets me for lunch every other Monday. I meet with Michelle on alternating Tuesday mornings for coffee. I've found that I have to be strategic in building friendships—otherwise moments, heartaches, and celebrations are lost as I plow forward through my calendar.

Don't hesitate to get organized when it comes to connecting with friends. Creating a network of support requires effort.

2 MORE THAN ONE

My seventeen-year-old daughter, Sam, told me the other day, "I have only one best friend, Mom. She is all I need."

Not twenty-four hours later, her only best friend started going out with a boy. Suddenly, Sam had a wide-open gap in her social calendar and a busy signal when she wanted to talk. Life felt very lonely. The same thing can happen to us. We need more than one close friend.

It's healthy and appropriate to have a few different friends to lean on throughout the stressful seasons of our lives. My husband has a friend he meets with for coffee, another with whom he climbs mountains. He also has some e-mail prayer buddies and an accountability partner.

If you have only one friend as your sole support, take a moment to think of one other person you would enjoy spending time with. Pick up the phone and set up a lunch. It's that easy to begin building a network.

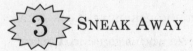 3 SNEAK AWAY

Is your calendar full over the next few months? Mine too. But if you pull it out right now, pick a weekend two months out, and plan in advance, you can set up a great girls' or guys' weekend getaway. Life will come at you either way, stressful situations will mount up, but if you have a time of refreshment scheduled, you'll be that much better prepared to handle the hardships.

You don't have to spend a lot of money either—lots of churches and retreat centers offer discounted rooms for those in the midst of a difficult season. Head off into the hills with someone you trust, take a hike, journal your thoughts, engage in conversation. Do something that will take you out of your current environment and place you in an out-of-the-way spot where you can focus on one of the great delights of life—friendship.

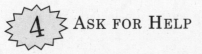 ASK FOR HELP

Since I've written the introduction to this book, we've moved. We moved from a two-bedroom to a three-bedroom apartment to accommodate our adult son moving in with us. It was a short-notice move, and I was embarrassed to invite friends over to help. I didn't want them to see the dust behind the television or the four boxes of half-used open spaghetti boxes in my cupboard. I'd had friends help me move before, but only after everything was boxed and tidy.

But I needed help.

Seven folks showed up, including spouses of friends. In other words, a few people I didn't even know! I was mortified by the dust bunnies and sticky refrigerator door...but they were not. They pitched in with smiles, loading boxes and food, cleaning out the old place and setting up the new one. It made the job a thousand times easier, and shockingly, not one of them shunned me for my frivolous spaghetti usage or my dust-bunny village.

You'd be surprised how much people want to help and how little they care about the things we worry about.

Ask. Think of one thing you need help with, and ask.

 ## 5 VENT

Pour it all out. Vent. I can "let it all hang out" with two of my friends. They know my heart, they know my longings, and with them, I am safe to simply speak the fears, worries, anger, and frustration that I may hide from other people. I have a few friends who do the same with me. I can usually hear it in Jennifer's voice when she just needs an ear. In those moments, she doesn't want or need advice; she just wants to get out the emotion so she can see things clearly.

We need that. Sometimes there is so much stuff cluttering our brains that a good venting session can help us sort through to the heart of it.

Do you have a safe friend in your life? This is definitely one of those therapeutic outpourings best reserved for someone you can trust. If you don't have a friend like that, I encourage you to keep reaching out, keep scheduling lunch and coffee dates, keep building until you get there.

 LISTEN

My jaw dropped as my friend shared the most recent news in her family saga. "You're kidding!" I said. "She said that?" She went on to share the latest in a series of tough conversations with members of her extended family. Tears came to her eyes as she talked of the hurt and heartache…and somehow, in the midst of hearing her story, I completely forgot my own troubles.

Being there for our friends makes a difference. Not only do we get to hear what is going on in the life of someone we care about, but we can be the shoulder to lean on in the hurt. With that comes a sense of value and purpose that stewing over our own problems just doesn't offer. While it's good to do the talking, also take some time to ask about and listen to the lives of your friends. Focus on what they might need in that moment. Truly listen. As you listen, you'll find your own issues, worries, and fears fading into the background.

7 ⬥ SHARE A MEAL

I put way too much pressure on myself when having friends over. I like the house to be perfect and the food to be top-notch—which explains why we don't have friends over near enough. Yet a shared meal is a wonderful way to forget about the pressures of the day and celebrate relationships. Don't worry about crafting the perfect meal, just order some pizzas on a Friday night and invite a few friends over. Linger around the table, visit about one another's week, find out where your friends grew up or what their funniest childhood memories are. After dinner, watch a movie together, play a card game, or pull out the Monopoly board.

For many of us, our tendency when we face stress is to

hunker down and stop hanging out with friends. In all reality, this is a time when we need friends the most.

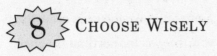 ## 8 CHOOSE WISELY

I've had a variety of friends over the years. In one season of my life, it seemed like all my friends were a little rough around the edges. Instead of encouraging me to do good things, they would say stuff like, "Hey, forget about it! Let's go get drunk tonight." Mmm. Don't think so. Even today, though my life is in a far different place, there are those who encourage the negative in me and those who bring out the positive. I try to stay away from people who encourage me to gossip or who point out all the worst-case scenarios.

On the flip side, I also stay away from those who give me quick solutions and spout spiritual niceties. Instead, I try to surround myself with authentic people of faith who listen to my heart and meet me where I am—with neither broken solutions nor religious clichés.

Choose wisely who you let into the inner places of your heart. You want to walk with people who will lovingly listen, let you vent, and then gently turn you toward truth.

9 CHEER 'EM ON

Once you've built a network of friends, be intentional about cheering each other on. Sometimes we focus so much on what is stressful or worrisome that we don't dedicate enough time to celebrating. Throw a party when someone gets a job. Sing for your friend when she gets the house cleaned. Buy lunch for your buddy when he climbs that mountain he's dreamed of conquering. Celebrate the big and little moments of success in one another's lives.

I made it through the day without chocolate the other day—my friend did the no-chocolate dance for me. She wiggled and grooved—and I laughed out loud. Celebration cultivates joy, and joy gives us the strength to face the reality of hardship ahead.

10 USE EVERY MEANS

Spending time with friends is a wonderful way to offset stress and worry. Being real, engaging in each other's lives— all are worthwhile objectives. Another way to build those friendships is to utilize the social technology available. You can update friends on Facebook or send out prayer requests via e-mail. If you are battling an illness, there are Web pages designed to send out updates to friends and family (check with your local hospital or doctor to find out more). Sending out a 911 text message to prayer partners is another quick way to connect with help whenever you need it. Some avoid social technology because they prefer face-to-face contact. That's great—I fully agree—but don't be afraid to use what's available to enhance your relationships.

11 SEEK COUNSEL

I'm not very good at asking for advice. It's that pride thing. I feel that asking for advice makes me look like I don't know what I'm doing. And since I want people to think I know what I'm doing…you see my dilemma. Sure, I'm growing out of it as I realize how little I actually do know and how little that matters, but it's been a process.

One huge benefit of good friends is to be able to ask their advice. Stress can cloud your vision. Before making any decision, ask your friends and others you trust and see what they say. Proverbs 15:22 says that many counselors make for successful decision making. That's a truth we can lean into.

12 Rally a Prayer Team

I recently received an e-mail from a dear friend who is deal-ing with huge stress in her world. She invited me to be part of her prayer team. She made it guilt-free; giving all her friends the freedom to say no if they were too busy. For those who answered yes, she now sends out a daily e-mail letting us know how we can pray on that day.

We can do the same. Reach out to your friends and in-vite them to stand with you in prayer. If they can't, be under-standing. We can't all do everything. For those who can participate, take advantage of their kindness and invite their prayers as you need them. You'll not only have that prayer covering, but you'll also have the incredible sweet sense that you are not alone.

13 Freedom to Be

One of my dear friends, Carol, lives seven hundred miles away. What I especially love about her is that I don't have to say a word, and it's just fine. Carol and I can enjoy a com-fortable silence that nurtures my heart. I don't have to talk deep things, crack funny jokes, or ask questions to start a conversation. I can just be.

Just this week I scheduled a girls' overnight with Carol. We'll meet somewhere in the middle of our seven hundred miles and hang out. Just be. I can't wait.

Do you have a friend with whom you can be completely still? And be okay? If not, I encourage you, once again, to continue building that network of relationships until that just-be friend finds her way into your world.

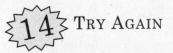 ## 14 TRY AGAIN

One final thought on friendship: it could be that you've been burned by a good friend. Maybe someone betrayed, rejected, or abandoned you. The thought of building friendships adds a whole new layer of stress to your world. Can I encourage you to take that hurt to God? Pour it out to him. Vent your anger. Lay it at his feet…and then, try again. Friendship is too vital, too important to toss aside. Yes, some people will hurt you, and some will walk away. But others will not. There are those who will stand with you through thick or thin. Don't miss those treasured companions because of a bad experience. It is a risk to trust others, but it is a risk worth taking.

SUMMARY

No one is meant to walk alone through life. This painful journey is best walked in the company of good friends—people who will laugh, cry, vent, and grow with you through life's adventures. I encourage you to invest time in these critical lifelines. Follow through on that lunch date, make the phone call, plan a weekend away, or rally your prayer team. Flip back through the last few pages. What is one action step you can take to build your friendship base? Don't delay—take that step today.

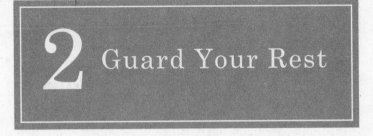

2 Guard Your Rest

He makes me lie down in green pastures, he leads
me beside quiet waters, he restores my soul.

—PSALM 23:2–3

Rest is one of the first things to fly out the window when stress builds in our lives. We stay up worrying, working, plotting, or planning. We stare at the ceiling and wonder what tomorrow will bring. We toss and turn. If we are blessed to get a full night's sleep, the day's emotions are so draining that we find ourselves never fully refreshed.

There's a solution. Guard your rest—even more so in the difficult seasons of life. Read through this next session with an open mind. Obviously you won't be able to utilize every suggestion, but if you can take one or two or six of these ideas and give them a shot, you'll be well on your way to finding rest.

 Nap Often

Even if it's only fifteen minutes, it's a great thing to lie down, stretch out, and close your eyes. I commit to doing this often, but if I'm honest, I find that it actually only happens once a week. When I worked from home, it was a little easier to nap after lunch, closing my eyes for ten or fifteen minutes. Today I work in a cubicle. Lying down doesn't go over well, and snoring is even worse. I've found this out the hard way.

So we obviously have to be realistic. If you work a full-time job and have to wait until you get home from work, great. If you're like me and a family is depending on you to connect and prepare a meal after work, then maybe take a little rest time after dinner. If that's unrealistic, then give yourself Sunday afternoon to shut the door, stretch out, and close your eyes. In other words, don't let this be another to-do item that leaves you frustrated because you can't check it off the list. Just keep in mind the value of rest and nap when you can.

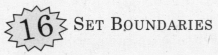 Set Boundaries

Setting boundaries with other people always sounds so emotionally healthy, so wise. Any one of us could probably attest to its benefit. But to actually do it? Not as easy.

Setting boundaries begins with understanding the emotional drain of whatever situation you're walking through. With our son in need of a kidney transplant, I know that my emotional and physical well of energy will be tougher to maintain—especially after the surgery. In anticipation of that, I'll keep speaking and writing engagements to a minimum and eliminate other things that might draw on that energy.

In the moments when I struggle to cut back my schedule, I have to remember where my value comes from. My value is not dependent on a full calendar and high visibility. I have to remind myself of that. You may too. Whatever fills your calendar today—do you know the heart and motive behind your choices? If your busyness is tied to your value, you may have to identify and work through those issues so that you can more easily say no.

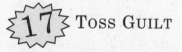 Toss Guilt

Kill the voice. You know the one I'm talking about. Yours may sound suspiciously like your mom or dad, a grade school teacher, or an older sibling. It's the internal voice that says, *You shouldn't be resting; you have too much to do. Why are you sitting still? You don't have time to sit still. You know, you're wasting the day away. What have you accomplished today? Nothing? Why not?*

We all battle the voice that tells us we're simply not doing enough. But battle we must. The voice is lying. You will be far more productive if you take the time to rest, refresh, and restore. And even if you're not more productive, you will certainly be better company to yourself and those you love. Guilt over much-needed rest is a universal weight we bear. But together, by affirming rest to one another and by living it each day, we can toss the guilt and get the refreshment we need. Start today by identifying that guilt-ridden accusing tone and eliminating it from your thoughts.

 BREATHE

I used to smoke cigarettes. For a long time, whenever I was stressed, I would step outside and smoke. I remember a dear friend once asking me, "Do you think you smoke just so that you'll breathe deeply once in a while? More than nicotine, is your body craving nice, slow deep breaths?"

Looking back, I think there may have been some truth

to her thought. When I smoked, it was the only time I would concentrate on breathing deeply, on inhaling. And I've come to notice that when I am stressed, I tend to breathe quicker, shallow breaths. Sometimes, simply breathing deep brings a certain calm to my heart. Try it. Right now, sit up straight and concentrate on breathing deeply, in and out. Try it for ten deep breaths.

See? I told you it helps!

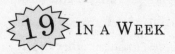

19 IN A WEEK

It's only one day a week. God calls it the Sabbath—a day set aside for rest and renewal. Amazing how few of us hold to this command. In our society, we've created a mind-set where it almost seems noble to set aside the Sabbath command in order to work. Yet God takes it very seriously. He himself chose to rest after creating the world; surely we can do the same after our workweeks! Carve out the Sabbath. One day a week to stay in your jammies, read a good book, go to church, hang out with friends. One day a week to set aside the worries and cares of the day and enjoy family.

I've used the same excuses, such as, *But I don't have time to rest this week.* Truthfully, you don't have time *not* to rest this week. The Sabbath is designed to recharge your batteries so that you can face the week ahead with the energy it will require.

Here's a suggestion that has worked well for several of my friends. If you struggle with taking a Sabbath day, start by taking a Sabbath morning or Sabbath afternoon. Give yourself the freedom to relax for a few hours one day a week. Start small. Start this week. You'll notice the difference as you head into next week.

 IN A YEAR

When was the last time you took a vacation? I've heard it said that you should divert daily, withdraw weekly, abandon annually. Every day, take a few moments to yourself. Every week, honor the Sabbath. Every year, take a week away. Now, it could be that thinking of a vacation only adds to your stress today. Maybe the very thought of planning a trip makes your stomach turn. If so, jump to the twenty-first way, below. Don't let this be an added source of stress. But if your heart lightens at the thought of a vacation, if you can immediately envision yourself basking in the sun on a warm beach, camping in the park across town, or exploring tourist attractions one state over, then I encourage you to take some time to put it together. Even if you can't work it in for another six months, putting it on the calendar will give you something to look forward to, something to think and dream about.

21 ⬧ PUT YOURSELF IN TIME-OUT

There are moments when it feels like my head will explode. Either that or words will actually spill out of my mouth that should never reach human ears.

In recent years, I've learned to recognize when stress puts me in danger of short-circuiting or overreacting, so I can put myself into time-out before careless comments hurt the people I love. If you feel stretched to your limit, if your anger, frustration, or stress is about to boil over and burn those closest to you, put yourself in time-out. Walk into your bedroom, bathroom, or closet…and lock the door. Breathe deep. Take some time to organize your thoughts. This is what you might call "forced rest"—taking yourself out of a situation before it can get the better of you. Practice it the next time you feel yourself losing control.

 **Sit in Quiet**

My dad used to sit in his easy chair after work, put both hands on his knees, and close his eyes. The room would be quiet. One day I asked him what he did in the stillness.

"I meditate," he said.

"Meditate on what?" I asked.

"On the quiet," he replied.

Hmm. He later explained that it helped him to process his day if he could sit still and try *not* to think for ten minutes. "It seemed like the longest ten minutes in the world the first time I did it," he said. But the more he practiced, the more he was able to stop thinking about work, money, or the next big project and simply take a few minutes to rest his brain. Afterward, he felt like he could fully engage with us as his family.

It could be that for you, like my dad, it may be a helpful tool to not think—for ten minutes.

23 Stretch

One of the areas where many of us hold our tension is in the neck and shoulders. Try these simple exercises to relax those muscles:

- *Neck:* Sit up straight with your arms hanging loosely at your sides. Turn your head to the right, hold for five seconds. Then to the left. Repeat three times. Do the same thing tilting your head to the right, to the left, and forward.
- *Shoulders:* Sit up straight and place your right hand on your left shoulder. With your left hand, pull your elbow across your chest toward your left shoulder. Hold for ten seconds. Do the same thing on the other side. Then raise your arms over your head; gently pull one elbow toward the opposite shoulder. Hold for ten seconds.

Just focusing on stretching tight muscles can relax your body and calm your mind.

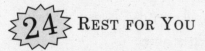 ## 24 REST FOR YOU

I love my time in the morning. I get up while it's still quiet, brew some coffee, and curl up on the couch. Then I read or journal or pray. I also love cuddling with my husband to watch a good movie—especially on a Friday night when I know the whole weekend lies in front of me.

What quiets your heart and
husband, watching college footl
for a hike is another way he reli
look like for you? It may be diff
your family. It doesn't matter. Yo
your own needs. Think of what rest might be for you,
go for it.

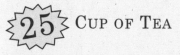 CUP OF TEA

Various experts espouse the health benefits of drinking tea. It's said that tea provides antioxidants, prevents heart disease, and fights cancer… I don't know about all those things, but I do know that in the time it takes to steep, sip, and savor a cup of tea, a few minutes of quality rest can be found. What if you commit to drinking one cup of tea a day—and during that time, you commit to doing nothing else? Simply taking the time to enjoy that one cup with no other distractions will give you fifteen to twenty minutes of quiet and rest each day.

The British are wise with their afternoon tea. It's a simple solution to savor the quiet.

A HELPING HAND

n't be afraid to encourage rest in one another. I do my best to encourage rest in my husband, and he does the same for me. Sometimes we just need a voice to speak truth to us. If you need that kind of help, invite a friend to be a rest-accountability partner. Check in with each other once a week to encourage quiet in each other's world. It could be that all you need is that extra little nudge to retreat and refresh.

SUMMARY

Setting aside time to rest can seem so frivolous—yet the benefits are God-ordained and irreplaceable. Is there a way you can incorporate rest into your world today? How can you divert daily, withdraw weekly, and abandon annually? What does rest look like to you? Take a few moments and flip through this section again. Pick out one thing you can do to be strategic about refreshment. Don't be shy, and don't let guilt enter into the equation. You need rest, friend. It will strengthen you for the days ahead.

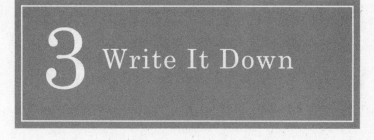

3 Write It Down

Trust in him at all times, O people;
pour out your hearts to him,
for God is our refuge.
—PSALM 62:8

I love the written word, and I seem to have a special knack for pouring out the stuff of life. I'm not talking about wise words or godly reflection; I'm talking about writing out hurt or fear in less-than-eloquent words. I once wrote in a hidden online journal that was so hidden, I have no idea where it is anymore. You can create an online blog and use maximum security settings so that it remains personal and private

Writing can be therapeutic. It clears out your brain so you can see things clearly. If you have never tried writing life down in order to walk through it, please give it a chance.

Even if you've tried it once before, try it one more time. Write through some of the following suggestions. You might discover a wonderful outlet to help you process both circumstance and emotion.

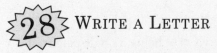27 VENT FREELY

Since I opened with venting, let's park there for a minute. Venting can be a great way to sift through life events. Without editing, pour out your heart. Write it in longhand, write it with a keyboard. Just write. Don't try to sound like you have it all together, and don't worry about flow. You can always toss it as soon as you're done. Jump from one subject to the next, wherever your pen leads you.

A great way to start this practice is to give yourself a five-minute time limit to write nonstop. Even if you start with "I don't know what to write…" just keep going. You may be surprised by where your writing leads, but that's okay. Sometimes you may vent to find you are angry or scared about something you never would have imagined. Well, then you can look at that later and apply truth, talk to a friend, and move through it. But if you never vent it out in the first place, you may not discover what's stirring underneath the pain.

28 WRITE A LETTER

If part of your stress and worry comes from a broken relationship, it can be incredibly helpful to write a letter. This isn't necessarily the type of letter you send, but it is the kind of letter that will help you process your emotions. When I went through a divorce, I experienced a wealth of emotions I could barely contain. On several occasions, I wrote all my feelings to my ex-husband. I never sent the letters, but it was amazing how it helped just get rid of the anger and sadness I experienced.

This is especially helpful if you have someone from your past whom you haven't forgiven. Writing a letter to that person and expressing all your hurt (whether you send it or not) can be a great first step in the healing process.

29 WRITE THE DAY

In a season of intense stress or worry, it helps to just write out the day. Write what happened, how you felt about it, what might lie ahead tomorrow. Not only will it help you in the moment, but it will also become a memorial. Years from now, you can look back to see what happened, how it all unfolded, and the lessons that you learned.

When I reflect on the years of being a single parent, the seasons start blurring together. But I can still go back to my journals and see the many ways that God met me, the friends who walked alongside me, the trials we moved through. It builds my faith and my sense of security in the truth that, ultimately, things are going to be okay.

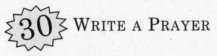 WRITE A PRAYER

I talk differently to God when I write to him. I end up addressing different things in different ways. I'm not sure why that is; I just know it to be true. If you've never written a prayer to God, take a portion of your journal and write out what's on your mind in letter form. Watch what unfolds.

Also, the wonderful thing about penning your heart to God is that you can look back and see how he has responded. Written prayers give us the chance to see that he truly does answer the cries of our hearts—even if it's not always in our timing.

 PEN HOPE

What do you hope will come from this season? I'm not talking about what your dreams might be; we'll discuss that a little later. But what do you hope will specifically come from this time in your life? Do you hope to become a stronger person? More full of grace? Do you hope to come through on the other side without punching anyone in the nose? What is it that you want to see from this? By writing it down, you give your brain something to shoot for, something positive to look toward.

What do you hope for?

32 PLASTER TRUTH

I've gone through seasons where I can barely see myself in the bathroom mirror because I've plastered note cards with God's promises all over the place. The bathroom mirror is one place where I can read them every day.

Sometimes we just need to remind ourselves of the truth. You can do the same. If there are financial worries, look up God's promises of provision. If you struggle with illness, write of God's healing and comfort. If you're facing relational heartache, plaster God's love all over your home. God is not disconnected from what you are going through. He is right there, right in the middle of it. By writing down his promises and his character, you give yourself a daily reminder that you are not facing any of this alone.

 Reminisce

Hamburgers, applesauce, and potato chips. There is no better taste in all the world. When I was a child, we would go camping or out for picnics, and it seemed like a lunch of hamburgers, applesauce, and potato chips was always the menu. I loved playing all morning and then gathering together to eat our lunch. I'd balance the paper plate (which was getting soggier by the minute) on my lap, munch on chips that had fallen into the applesauce, and grin a toothless smile at my brothers.

It was a simple pleasure that still brings me joy. What sweet childhood memory sits in your mind? Take some time and write down some good memories. They might be just what the doctor ordered.

34 Build a Story

Gather together family or friends or anyone really. Jot down the first line to a story. Have the next person write another line or two. Pass the sheet around with each person writing one or two lines to the story.

Read it out loud.

Laugh uncontrollably.

Banish worry.

My daughter, Sam, and I did this once on a long plane ride. She started the story, and we went back and forth for nearly an hour. After a few pages, we read it out loud to each other. We laughed so hard, the flight attendants came by and gave us their quit-being-so-loud glare.

Playfulness is a great antidote for worry, stress, or long plane rides.

 IMAGINE

Write what it would look like to move past the current issue that is causing frustration. Envision how it would feel to be out of debt, feeling better, or in a restored relationship with someone you love. Go into detail and build scenarios. Sometimes by imagining the future (and writing it down), you can gain just enough inspiration to make it through today.

36 PRAISE

Shepherd. Provider. Mighty. Holy one. Rescuer. Strength. Life. God is all these things and more. When we take the time to acknowledge him, to write down what we love about him—something happens in our hearts. We recognize that not only is he all these things, but he is all these things in *our* lives. In other words, he will shepherd our kids. He'll provide for our needs. He is mighty to save. He is holy and trustworthy with our broken hearts. He will rescue and give us strength. He, no matter what is swirling around us, is our life. Praise opens the door to the truth that we belong to a God who loves us deeply and stands with us completely.

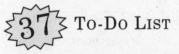 TO-DO LIST

I could barely get to sleep. Everything I needed to do sifted in and out of my thoughts, a never-ending to-do list. I was afraid I would forget to do one thing and the rest of the list would fall apart. So over and over, I processed what I needed to do next. Finally, after another few sleepless hours, I climbed out of bed, grabbed a pen, and wrote out my to-do list. I put everything I could think of onto that paper, fell back into bed, and was out like a light.

Sometimes it helps just to write it all down.

 38 ANSWER QUESTIONS

I need help figuring out what I feel. Some emotions are tucked away so deep, I don't even know what they are, where they come from, or how I can move forward. I'll know that they're there, because they come out in different ways, but there are times I get stuck trying to identify them. If the same thing happens to you, it can help to ask some simple questions and then journal—again, without editing and without worrying about anyone else reading it. Ask yourself: What am I feeling right now? What situation/circumstance takes up most of my thought life? Why? What am I scared of? What is the truth? Start with these questions and then write as long as your pen and your heart will allow. You might be surprised by what you discover about yourself.

39 GRATITUDE

When I'm stressed, the last thing I want to do is look at the good. It's tough to try to think positive when things feel like they are crumbling around you. But it makes a difference. When I first started my gratitude journal, my list was very small. But still, at the end of every day, I tried to write down three things I was grateful for. They were often simple things: a warm shower, a decent meal, my daughter's smile. But the more I focused on the good, the harder it was to stay entrenched in worry and the more likely I was to imagine a positive outcome.

40 PRAYER REQUESTS FOR OTHERS

Write down what God is doing in the lives of those you love. Just today, I heard some friends share how God helped them through a difficult season recently. It touched my heart and gave me strength. It reminded me that God will not abandon me.

By writing down prayer requests (and answers) for those you love, you can document how God is moving in their lives—which will give you the sweet reminder that he is also working in yours.

41 WRITE A THANK-YOU NOTE

Thank the people who support you today. Thank the people who have supported you in the past. There is something about that heart of thankfulness that will help you focus on what people have done to come alongside you. Especially if you've been betrayed or abandoned by someone you care about, thanking those who have not walked away can be just the thing to pull you out of a funk.

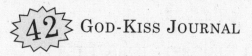 GOD-KISS JOURNAL

I take sunsets personally. A bright moon on a clear night is another example of God's specific love. Like a bouquet of roses from a dear friend, kisses from God brighten my world. The same is true for you. The song that speaks to your heart, the beauty that captures your eye, the anonymous check in the mailbox, or the hug right when you need it—God will make his love real to you in a thousand different ways, all according to your specific wiring. First, ask him for eyes to see, then jot down the ways he shows you his presence. As pages fill up with his care, you'll be able to move through this season with confidence, knowing you are loved and carried by the good and gracious Savior of the world.

SUMMARY

The written word is said to be a powerful source of encouragement, enlightenment, and education. Whether you take the time to pen your prayer requests or you pour out your hurting heart on paper, writing it down will grant you a new perspective. You'll actually be writing your own history, and through that you will see God's hand, your growth, and maybe even gain insights into how all the pieces fit together. You'll also have the chance to empty out the jumble of thoughts in your brain, freeing up your mind to deal with the here and now. Incorporate a few of the ideas listed in this chapter—journaling, writing letters, compiling a God-kiss list—and see what happens as you put pen to paper.

4 Dream a Little

There is surely a future hope for you,
and your hope will not be cut off.

—PROVERBS 23:18

I can imagine it—my cabin by the water. I picture the deck.
I see the rowboat pulled up on shore. My fishing pole hangs
over the edge—ready at a moment's notice to capture wrig-
gling, gleaming, championship fish. I can envision the
touching moment of scooping up my first bass, kissing his
gills, thanking him for the challenge, and setting him free.

It brings me joy just thinking about it.

Which is why I'm devoting a section to dreaming.
There's nothing like a little daydreaming to dispel the cob-
webs of worry and stress. You'll find a series of questions
under each heading. Whether you pull out a piece of paper
or sit and daydream over a cup of coffee, have fun with it.

 To Live

If you could live anywhere, where would you live? What country? What state? What would your home look like? Would you live by the water or near a mountain? Would you have a deck? Lots of windows? Or would you prefer an underground bunker? Go on, have fun with it.

I love thinking about this. For most of my life, I'd never considered where I might want to live or what kind of home I would enjoy. I'd simply taken on the desires, dreams, and hopes of the people in my world. When I finally sat down to imagine what I would love, my cabin popped into my brain. I still don't have it, but I do enjoy thinking about it as a someday possibility. Remember, this isn't an exercise in materialism, in imagining what you could have if only… Instead, it's an exercise in discovering who you are and what you like. It's giving your heart something to dream about and work toward. And that can only be a good thing.

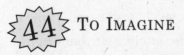 To Imagine

What do you want to be when you grow up? What is your dream job? If you could do anything in the whole wide world, no limits or conditions, what would you do? This doesn't have to have anything to do with your current career (unless, of course, it's your dream job). Take a few minutes and really think it through. What is your passion? What brings you joy?

Once you think through the questions, pause for a moment. Is there one step you can take to bring you closer to that dream? One thing you can do to create the opportunity? You never know, all this dreaming could lead you down the path of fulfilling what God has had in mind for you all along.

 ## To Meet

If you could meet anyone, whom would you want to meet? Why? Is there someone in your local circle...a pastor, a local politician, a businessperson, or respected family man or woman with whom you've thought, *I'd like to have lunch with him or her.* If so, why not give it a shot? There's no huge risk in giving someone a call or sending an e-mail. Invite a person you admire out for coffee or lunch. If your first invite can't make it, try again. Expanding your world is a great way to see beyond the stresses of the here and now.

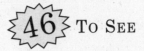 **TO SEE**

There are all kinds of museums along I-70 on my way from Colorado to Missouri. I've traveled past them a hundred times but have never stopped. There's the sign that boasts, "See the Live Six-Legged Steer!" There's another sign encouraging me to exit so I can take a picture of the biggest ball of twine and another with a museum commemorating a pioneer I've never heard of, but who obviously did something cool enough to be touted on I-70.

Someday I'm going to drive through Kansas and stop to see every sight advertised. Truly, how could my worries not fade into the background after witnessing the valiant life struggle of a six-legged steer or a town rallying around the biggest ball of twine ever?

What do you want to see? What tourist attraction? state? animal? friend? world wonder? Think about it. Dream of it. Is there a unique roadside attraction in your future?

47 **TO EXPERIENCE**

I was strapped to a man I didn't know, traveling at speeds I couldn't calculate, falling from a height I could barely fathom. I was skydiving, and I'd dreamed of doing it since I was a little girl.

Well, you may think, *I don't have the money/time/courage to pursue that kind of adventure.* Don't think like that. I went skydiving as a single mom with no income. I was literally on welfare, and yet God opened a door, provided the means, and in the midst of a tough season of life, I got to experience one of my lifelong dreams. What would you like to experience? Have you always wanted to ski? scuba dive? hike a mountain? run a marathon? eat exotic cuisine? Think of something completely random and have fun imagining it. You never know, God could have it for you right around the corner. And there's nothing like dreaming of a little adventure to see you through the worries of today.

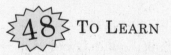 TO LEARN

I've always wanted to learn how to take a good photo. I'd like to take a course on making movies, and I wouldn't mind exploring how to paint a halfway decent picture. Sure, I know we won't have the money to do these things anytime soon, but I can start learning by checking out Web sites and gaining whatever base knowledge I need.

What would you like to learn? Have you always wanted to know about classical paintings? Is there an instrument you'd like to play? Think of ten things you would like to learn over the next decade. Then when you have some downtime, do a little research. A great way to take your mind off today is by stretching your brain to learn new things tomorrow.

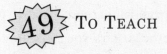 To Teach

What do you know that others don't? You have your own wealth of expertise. Now, don't scoff. It's true. No one has walked the path you have walked. No one has done the things you've done. And guess what? There is someone who wants to know, someone you can teach.

My husband and I just signed up to help lead a class for divorced people. Do we have a lot on our plate? Yes. But there is something about connecting and teaching others that feeds our hearts. For some of you, that may only be a drain—especially in a difficult season. You know yourself best. If pouring into others energizes you, consider what you may have to offer those who are on the path you have already traversed.

50 To Savor

I watch what I eat. Oh sure, there are times I ignore calories and fat, but I'm at the stage where I know better, so I almost always feel guilty for indulging. And yet food is one of the good gifts God gives to us, and there were times in the Bible when he ordained festivals where all who attended simply enjoyed the prepared feast.

When was the last time you ate something and lingered over the taste? Can you remember the last time you enjoyed planning a feast without thinking of how it would impact your waistline?

What kind of food do you enjoy? Plan a meal for this coming weekend, a meal of your favorite foods. Prepare it with someone you love, and don't allow guilt to creep in. Without overdoing it, savor the taste, the moment, the gift of good food.

51 To Grow

What is one area of your life where you'd like to grow and mature? Do you want to become more patient? wiser?

more fun to be around? What aspect of your world would you like to address? Now, this is not a time to beat up on yourself or think of what you don't like about yourself. Think in the positive. What type of person would you like to become? If you could pick one area to grow in, what would it be? And what is one practical step that could get you moving in that direction? It might be reading a book on the topic or talking to an expert. Think what you would like to grow through and then take a small step toward that end. You'll feel better just for moving forward.

52 TO CHANGE

Just for the sheer joy of dreaming, what would you do to change the world? If you were given full reign and all power, what would you do to make the world a better place? The fun thing about dreaming along these lines is that you just may discover what God has planted as a passion in your heart. Dream. You are king or queen of the world—what would you do to bring hope to the hurting masses?

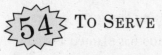

53 TO LOVE

Nothing alleviates stress and worry like allowing love to consume your thoughts. I'm not talking about romantic love, though that can be a part of it. I'm talking about simply loving other people. I once asked God to give me eyes to see people as he sees them. I found myself delighting in the smile of a friend or the voice of a singer or the words of an author. I felt a deep appreciation for the people around me—and while focusing on why I loved the people dearest in my life, I found it difficult to hold on to my fear of what might come next in my own world. Somehow, when we are able to take our eyes off ourselves and celebrate the beauty in someone else, it makes a difference. Who is close in your world? What do you love about them? Think of it—and if you start feeling really wild and crazy, tell them.

54 TO SERVE

If you could serve anyone, whom would you serve? Would you serve the homeless, bringing them a warm meal at night? Would you open your door to the divorced? the ill? the lonely? Who stirs your heart? I like to help hurting women. I long to come alongside them and meet them at their point of need. If I could, I would remind each one of the Father's love. Dreaming of that makes me smile. What makes you smile? Imagining ways you can impact the lives of others will change how you view your current circumstances. Everything you go through becomes part of the path to serving others. Whatever you are experiencing right now can become part of a powerful tool kit in taking care of others. Knowing that may help you walk through the hardship of today.

SUMMARY

Sometimes we forget to dream. One of the greatest losses to come from worry and stress is the way it can strip our hearts of the ability to imagine anything better around the corner. That's what this section is all about—focusing on the future, on dreams, on something other than the heartache of the here and now. Maybe it was tough for you to think through the ideas in this chapter. Perhaps you've stepped away from wondering what you want to do, see, become. Can I just encourage you? As long as you have breath, you can dream. It doesn't matter how old you are, what you've walked through, what might be going on right now. Dreaming of the future can bring new life to the present. Glance back through the ideas, and try one on for size. Dream a little.

5 Find the Humor

A cheerful heart is good medicine.
—PROVERBS 17:22

It gets serious around my home. In trying to navigate government health programs, dialysis for our son, finances, and our daughter's teenage heartaches, we can spend a lot of time figuring it out. Life feels heavy, and humor doesn't come easily. But we need it. Laughter is not only medicinal for the heart, it is a documented health benefit—it's good for the body too.

This section will share some ideas to incorporate humor into life. Skip over those that don't fit you and give the other ones a chance. Work up a good belly laugh, let the tears come to your eyes as you guffaw a time or two. It will do your heart and your body good.

 In Family

Family is defined in lots of different ways. You don't have to be married with kids to enjoy family. It could be you're still single and your family is made up of parents, siblings, and cousins. For those without biological family, even really good friends in the faith can become like family. And there's nothing like family to get you laughing. Set aside an evening for fun questions. Circle up in the living room and try these to get you started:

- What has been your most embarrassing family moment?
- What was your funniest childhood fight? With siblings, friends, or a teacher?
- What was your goofiest mishap at a family gathering?
- What was your family's favorite animal growing up? Do you have a silly pet memory?

Get creative with questions and answers. Have fun with it and watch how connected you feel after an evening of telling stories.

56 · IN RANDOM CHILDREN

If you don't have kids in your life, find some. Volunteer in your Sunday school; baby-sit a neighbor's child. Little ones know how to laugh, and if you allow yourself to enter their world, you'll join them in their joy. Right around Christmastime, my husband and I went to the mall and watched the children as they prepared to sit on Santa's lap. Some went with enthusiasm and spilled out a long list of wants they'd obviously been memorizing for weeks; others went screaming and kicking while parents tried to make them smile with antics they'd normally reserve for the privacy of their home. We couldn't help but laugh as we watched. I'm smiling even now.

And I promise you, if you have any close friends with preschoolers, they'll be more than willing to lend you a child or two for an evening. In fact, they may even pay you for the privilege.

57 · IN *READER'S DIGEST*

Every month, my family eagerly anticipates *Reader's Digest*. Yes, of course there are good stories to warm the heart and inspire our dreams, but we like the jokes best. Sam will see the magazine in the mailbox and immediately the next few hours are set in stone. We'll sit in the living room and read different funnies out loud to each other, taking turns. There have even been a few jokes that have stayed with us to be repeated over the years. It's such a simple way to laugh together.

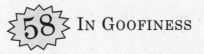 58 IN GOOFINESS

My niece recently wrote how devastated she was after her first breakup. At twelve years old, it was a tough thing to walk through. I live far away and knew her parents would counsel her with all wisdom and grace.

So I decided to add a touch of humor.

I wrote Mary a poem:

Boys are yucky, yes they are,
  boys are yucky, near and far.
Boys are yucky, they break our hearts,
  boys are yucky, they burp and fart.

Mary wrote me back with a big smiley face, "Thanks, Aunt Elsa. That's just what I needed!"

I do the same with my girl. "Sam," I'll say, "wanna hear a poem?"

She'll look at me, a little twinkle in her eye. "No, not really."

I'll tell it to her anyway.

Totally random. Totally goofy.

And we laugh.

Feeling poetic? It may be just what the doctor ordered.

59 IN THE NEWS

I think there must be something twisted in my thinking. When I scroll through the news, I'm often captured by the worst in human nature. Why do I choose to read the story of the homicidal maniac or teenagers gone bad and then wonder why my outlook has become more pessimistic?

The reality is there are all kinds of laugh-worthy things in the news. From thieves who leave their ID's behind to misspelled ads to political antics. Choose to search out only the funny stories, and spend some time enjoying the oddities in our world. If there isn't anything to draw a good laugh, turn to the comics. If that doesn't work, subscribe to a news feed that fills you in on funnier stories of crooks gone goofy. There's plenty of bad news. Maybe it's time to divert your attention to happier fare.

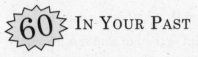 ## 60 IN YOUR PAST

Reminisce about funnier times. When I married my husband, Brian, we honeymooned on a tropical island. Little did we know the place we chose was somewhat clothing optional. I remember our first sighting. We were walking down the beach, and in the distance a couple was walking toward us. As they drew closer, we looked at them, looked at each other, turned bright red, and quickly found something interesting to observe on the horizon. On one occasion, a couple walked toward us fully clothed. We sighed in relief. Then as they drew nearer, in one svelte movement the gentleman tore off his apparently Velcro bathing suit.

We quickly learned to simply stand and smooch each time people wandered near. Even now, as I think of the gentleman with the Velcro suit, I laugh out loud.

You've walked through funny circumstances, either alone or with those you love. Think back. Enjoy it one more time.

 IN YOURSELF

I'm quirky. One of my more recent quirks occurs when my husband is driving. I've been in a few car accidents lately, so I now gasp every time someone hits his brakes in front of us. Seriously. Nearly every time. I've tried to stop this involuntary intake, but it doesn't seem to work. Some part of my brain sees brake lights and yells, "NOW! WE'RE GOING TO CRASH RIGHT NOW!" And I gasp.

Initially, I would just get irritated with myself, apologize to everyone in the car, and sulk about my malfunctioning "gasper." Not anymore. Now, I just laugh. I'll even get dramatic and add a few playful comments to lighten things up.

We all have our quirks. We can take ourselves too seriously and take quick offense, or we can laugh it off.

I say laugh.

62 IN DANCE

I have no rhythm. I haven't taken a single dancing lesson, and I don't know that I ever will. Okay, wait. I think I may have tackled country line dancing back in the day, but I'll be perfectly honest with you. It didn't work out.

And yet there is something about dancing randomly that just makes me laugh. Try it. Turn on some music and swing your tushie. Have a friend, child, or spouse pick a favorite song, and dance together in the living room. Pick one yourself. Unless dancing is your line of work, I guarantee a little twirl through the house will bring a smile to your face.

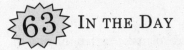 IN THE DAY

There had to be one funny thing that happened today. Maybe your child woke up with the craziest bed-head ever, or at work someone mismatched polka dots and stripes, or maybe the DJ on your favorite radio station made a funny observation. Ask God to let you see the humor in your world and then look with expectant eyes.

Prayerfully, you might just find a guffaw before sundown.

 IN JOKES

Subscribe to a daily joke e-mail. Check Google for funny, clean jokes. The other night my daughter found a Web site with all the best Christian jokes. She followed me around with the computer and read them off to me. We laughed for a good hour together.

Another option is to host a joke night with friends. Invite a few people over and instead of bringing snacks and drinks, task them with bringing their three favorite jokes. Enjoy a meal of pizza and alternate telling favorites.

 ## In Movies

Some movies are just designed to make us laugh. But if you're anything like me, you might find the current cultural fare not nearly as funny as the things you grew up with. So what about having a movie night with your favorite funny movies from childhood? Make a list of your top ten, stop by the video store, pop some popcorn, and make a night of it. Another idea is to allow family members to each choose their favorite funny movie. Watch a different favorite every Friday night.

66 In People

My daughter found a great Christian comedian through her friends. Together, we watched a dozen of his YouTube videos one evening. I laughed so hard, tears rolled down my cheeks. I think of Bill Cosby and his classic monologues that still draw peals of laughter, enough to make my tummy hurt. There are all kinds of clean comedians out there today. Do a little investigating and then enjoy…and be sure to pass the information around. We could all use a good, clean laugh.

67 In Friendship

My husband comes from a large family, and some of his best friends are his brothers. To see those guys watching a football game, you would think they were teenagers. They razz each other over every play, throw stuff across the room, and laugh deep belly laughs over cutting remarks.

My girlfriends don't cut each other down for a good laugh, but we have our own way of bringing out the humor in each other. I have one friend in particular who has her own unique perspective on life. With a totally straight face, she'll make a comment that catches us all off guard and sends us into rounds of laughter. Just spending time with Gretchen is a guarantee of a smile. Who brings that out in you?

Schedule some time with someone who makes your eyes crinkle in delight.

68 In Story

Humor writers are tough to come by but great fun to read. Ask some friends for writers they recommend. Pick up a lighthearted book, park yourself at a coffee shop, and spend an evening in a different world. If you're not a big reader, go chapter by chapter. Even reading a humor writer over the dinner table can spur conversation about the most mundane and yet delightful aspects of life.

69 In Play

Our family goes crazy over a game called Wizard. It's a card game that's pretty easy for any age player to learn. We've played it with our extended family or with just the four of us at the kitchen table. A good game always gets our competitive teasing going, which makes it all the more fun. Other games that bring out the silly side include charades (try progressive charades, it's a kick!), Guesstures, Cranium, and Pictionary. It's tough to focus on the hard stuff of life when you're acting out or attempting to draw a dancing elephant on roller skates.

Plan a game night with family and friends, and watch how the weight of the world rolls off your shoulders.

SUMMARY

Sometimes when worry and stress crowd our lives, we simply forget to laugh. Or truth be told, we just don't want to look at the lighter things of life. Grace on you, friend. I know it may seem silly to watch a goofy movie or read through the comics—especially when you may be in the midst of life-or-death circumstances. But keep this in mind—laughter doesn't strip away the gravity of what you're facing. It doesn't demean the heartache or make light of the stress. Laughter simply gives you a momentary break from the weight of it all. Give it a try. Pick one idea and implement it this weekend. You just might surprise yourself with how good you will feel.

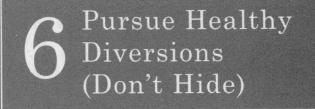

6 Pursue Healthy Diversions (Don't Hide)

If you, then, though you are evil, know how
to give good gifts to your children, how much
more will your Father in heaven give good
gifts to those who ask him!

—MATTHEW 7:11

When life gets painful, I hide in food. I'll think that a bag
of buttery popcorn or a guacamole burger will be just the
ticket to alleviate the pain.

And then it doesn't.

Not only does overeating *not* alleviate pain, it also adds
extra weight to hips that don't have room for expansion.

I don't know what your hiding place is—maybe drinking, pornography, reading too much, perfection—we all
have our broken default settings. Without awareness, any
one of the ideas in this section could become an unhealthy

hiding place. But by keeping God first and introducing healthy pursuits or occasional delights, God can use these gifts to give us a break from the pain.

Keeping balance in mind, here are a few ideas for healthy distractions.

 COOK

I never considered myself a cook. My greatest cooking feat included mac and cheese and the occasional boiled hot dog. But then I discovered a few great Web sites that make cooking a breeze—they offer detailed directions and careful measuring. I don't do well left to my own devices, so instructions are critical. Google "recipes" and you'll find many Web sites that offer different ideas; some even highlight cooking with just a few ingredients (for those of us undone by multiple spice combinations).

No matter what you choose, cooking a meal can be a fun distraction. Cooking with someone you love is even better. Invite a friend, recruit your spouse or child, and make it a family project. Enjoy your fine creation over a sit-down meal, and watch the stress of the day melt away.

 EXPLORE

When I was little, one of my favorite things to do was to get lost in the woods behind my house. I didn't have any great destination in mind, no grand hike from point A to point B; I just walked out my back door and lost myself in the tree stumps and wildflowers. Not too long ago, I did the same thing with my husband. We'd been in our home for two years and had yet to explore the woods behind the house. Finally, one warm Saturday afternoon, we scrambled down into the ravine, climbed over tree trunks, and explored our own backyard. It was so fun!

Wherever you live, whether in the city or out in the country, when was the last time you walked out the door with no real destination in mind? Go. Explore. You never know what you may find just around the corner.

 ## 72   MUSIC

What's your favorite type of music? Are you a country fan? classical? rap? jazz? What tunes get your foot tapping and your head bobbing? When I was younger, I would kick back and listen to music for hours—not so much anymore. Yet there's something therapeutic about allowing songs to wash over us and take us someplace, either into the rhythm or into the story being told. For a lot of us, music will bring back specific memories. Why not park there for a bit? Float back in time and allow the music to remind you of the sights and smells of yesterday. It may just give you the warm fuzzy gumption to tackle today.

 Fix

Nothing adds to stress like a dripping faucet, a cracked window, or a broken light bulb. Little irritants can become huge frustrations when you're at your limit emotionally. Create a to-do list of quick fixes, and then fix one thing every Saturday. If you're not a fix-it kind of person, ask around for friends who may be. It could be that these things could have been fixed long ago if you'd only asked. Why not ask now? In just a few weeks, minor irritants will be resolved, and you'll feel proud of yourself for taking care of the problem.

 Organize

This is not my strong suit. Even now, I glance around my desk to see piles of papers that have yet to be tackled. But I know myself. Once I do it, once I sit down and sift through and arrange every stray piece of paper, I always feel better. Same thing in my home. When everything has its place, and everything is in its place, I always feel so on top of things, like the teacher just planted a gold star on my forehead.

If you have trouble staying organized, use the ten-minute rule. Every day before you leave the office, take ten minutes to organize your desk. Every night before you go to bed, take ten minutes to organize your home. Those ten minutes will add up, and you'll enjoy the benefit of keeping things together.

 CLEAN

This may sound suspiciously like organization, but this is one step better. I can organize my desk, but I still have dust bunnies behind my picture frames. I can straighten up the kitchen at home and still have crumbs on the counter. Cleaning takes organization one step deeper, and it does a heart good.

I've shared already how our adult son has moved in with us. When we switched apartments, I cleaned the old place and straightened up the new one. It felt so good to get all the spots out of the carpet, dust the baseboards, and leave the empty refrigerator spotless. While I'm not a neat freak, it put me in good spirits to have everything looking good.

Now I do acknowledge that I'm a bit of an odd duck. If cleaning doesn't feel even remotely like a healthy distraction, don't let it be a weight. Try this—if you don't have the gumption to clean the whole house, start with something small, like the car. Somehow, driving around without fast-food bags or crumpled papers really does lighten your emotional load.

 EXERCISE

I've never met anyone who truly likes exercise. Oh, we all like the results and those fun little endorphins coursing through our systems, but very few people enjoy the actual act of exercising. For some reason, that knowledge helps me. It saves me from the expectation that in order to be svelte Nike chick, I have to look forward to sweating to the oldies. I don't look forward to it. But I'll still do it. I work out four to five times a week because I love the aftereffects. I like the sense of accomplishment it brings. Of course I'd like to add that I love how good my body looks, but since I still occasionally hide in buttery popcorn, I'm just not there yet.

What I do love is that no matter how stressed I am when I exercise, I walk out with a better outlook. And that helps.

77 HIGH SCHOOL MUSICAL (OR FOOTBALL)

This distraction is dependent on where you live. I lived in Arkansas for a season, and everyone in the community would turn out for a Friday-night football game. You'd see neighbors, friends, community leaders—all there to cheer on the team. Today I live in Colorado. Our high school football doesn't draw the big crowds, but soccer does. In some states, the high school plays and musicals are so topnotch that the whole community comes out to enjoy them. Whatever is popular in your area, go check it out. Get involved with the teenagers in your community. Support their games, watch their musicals, be a part of their world. As you sit and watch a fifteen-year-old sing her heart out or a seventeen-year-old throw the football with uncanny accuracy, your worries will quickly take a backseat for the evening.

78 COMPETE

It was the family reunion of 2002. I have four older brothers, and they decided to create a family Olympics at our reunion. In the months leading up to our time together, they ran, swam, and cycled their way to fitness. When the day finally came, they engaged in a little friendly competition with the whole family cheering them on. We even had medals to offer the winners.

What does some healthy competition have to do with stress? Well, several of my brothers went through tough things during their season of training—family heartache, work issues, other tensions—and the competition helped them focus on something beyond their current circumstances.

No, you don't have to orchestrate a family Olympics for all your siblings or friends, but you could look at entering a local triathlon (for whatever your age group) or a charitable 5K or anything else that will get you training your body and dreaming of something beyond today.

79 SET RANDOM GOALS

I made the list when I was in my early twenties—"one hundred things I want to do before I die." It included everything from skydiving to marrying the man of my dreams to eating frog legs. I have about thirty things left to do and, prayerfully, a good fifty years to make them happen. In fact, I may finish up the list sooner and start the whole process over again.

Make your own lifelong to-do list. Don't limit yourself; write down any- and everything you ever wanted to do. Set little goals and big goals, attainable and some that seem un-attainable. Have a few of your friends or family members complete their own lists too. Then share your ideas and help each other complete your goals.

80 CHILDHOOD PLEASURES

One of my favorite childhood pleasures came when my dad used to take our whole family to the ice-cream shop on the way home from a Saturday outing. I can picture the little store with the blue awning and the gravel parking lot. Every time, without question, I would get butter pecan ice cream on a sugar cone. One scoop, with rainbow sprinkles.

Mmm.

What were some of your childhood pleasures? Swinging on a swing? Watching a Disney movie? Building a tent in the living room and telling stories by flashlight? Hiking through the woods? Whatever they were, take a weekend to partake of those pleasures once again. You just might find that enjoying what made you smile as a child will bring you joy as an adult.

 READ

I was a nerd. Okay, I *am* a nerd. And as a little girl, my favorite thing to do was to go to the library and walk out with an armload of books. I read everything from the Hardy Boys (confiscated from my brothers) to teenage romance novels and action stories. I would absolutely lose myself in the adventures.

Today things are a little different. I rarely read fiction anymore. I more often read books on faith, personal growth, etc. Typically, I only get a good fiction book when I'm traveling, and I always feel a little guilty enjoying it.

Yet story is a powerful way to move out from our own circumstances and lose ourselves in a different world. On occasion, that's not a bad thing. Fiction can inspire, entertain, or distract. And when stress or worry crowd out your joy, a little adventurous distraction might be just the ticket.

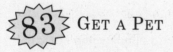

82 Savor This Sweet

We talked about cooking, we discussed my childhood love of butter pecan ice cream, but this is something different. This is all about chocolate, especially dark chocolate. It's documented that chocolate, in moderation, offers a distinct health benefit. Rich in antioxidants, dark chocolate has been known to lower blood pressure (source: webmd.com).

Feeling your blood pressure rise as life stress escalates? Savor this sweet. While it may not solve life's problems or lower blood pressure in your particular case, at the very minimum it will give you a few minutes of sheer delight as it melts on your tongue.

83 Get a Pet

Reeses Allan McGee. He's our nine-year-old golden retriever and one of my favorite confidantes. In my years as a single parent, I spent many evenings curled up around Reeses, crying into his fur or venting over the latest heartache. He would lick my tears or look at me in earnest response as I shared my day. It calmed my heart to pet Reeses, and when

I would come home from work, his wagging delight would bring instant joy.

While pets do add another to-do item to our lives, their companionship can be a source of great delight when we're facing tough times. Since Reeses was—and is—a big dog, he also needed lots of exercise. He became my inspiration to get out every day, into the sunshine—and while there were many days I did it solely for him, I ended up experiencing the benefits and rewards.

84 LOVE THIS MOMENT

I stood at the airport waiting for my husband to arrive from his business trip last night. My heart was heavy with all the worries for our son, our daughter, and our family. A young woman came up beside me. Her little two-year-old boy stared at me with big blue eyes. His blond hair was spiked, and he was in his most dapper outfit. His mom pointed toward the people coming toward baggage claim, "Watch for him, honey. Daddy's coming…"

I turned with them to watch. A few minutes later a man came our way. His hair was spiked too, his matching blue eyes twinkled. "There he is!" he exclaimed as he came and scooped up his son. I watched the boy giggle and clutch his daddy. I watched the mom kiss her husband hello. I let my heart celebrate their joy in each other. I felt a smile come and erase the furrow in my brow.

I whispered a thank-you to God for the portrait of joy that family represented and for the chance to taste their happiness and, for the moment, steal it as my own.

Lose yourself in the moments surrounding you. Someone else's joy may become your own.

85 ⟩ ENJOY ANOTHER'S GIFTS

I used to feel cheated when I observed the talent in others. Whether I listened to a great singer or read a great author, I would feel this jealousy rise up in my heart. I wanted to be good at something. I wanted to be the best at something— and my ambition made me envious and resentful of those who were accomplished in their craft.

No more.

Today I am so grateful for those who can communicate their heart through song. I delight in someone who can craft a story and capture my heart with fictional characters. I'm thankful for those who can put a meal together or who have that unique knack of making a house a home.

If you allow stress to build up through comparing your life to the lives of your friends, ask God to help give you clear vision and a thankful heart. Celebrating the gifts of others will ease the tension of a stressful world.

SUMMARY

There's any number of unhealthy ways to handle stress. Too much of anything can become a hiding place when we feel overwhelmed. But if we take time to cultivate healthy distractions, it can keep us from heading down a broken path. Take some of these ideas, sift through what works best for you, and run with it. Fight the temptation to think that you're strong enough that you don't need anything else to do or think about. It's not true. We all need to take a break from the hard realities of life and enjoy the good gifts God has given. It's okay. Get a pet, set some random goals, or go for a nice jog. Even tonight, think for a moment, what can you do to take care of you?

7 Dive into Truth

My comfort in my suffering is this:
Your promise preserves my life.
—PSALM 119:50

I've heard it said that 90 percent of what we worry about
never happens. I see that in my own life. I may start the day
worrying about making my mortgage, work up to worry
over kids, marriage, car trouble, accidents, acts of God, etc.,
and round out the evening with worry over whether the next
day will carry as much worry as today. It's exhausting, and
most of my fears never come to pass. There's hope. Once we
recognize how much we worry, we can take the much-
needed step of applying truth to our fears. Clinging to truth,
talking ourselves through to truth, reminding ourselves of
the truth—it all makes a difference.

Here's what applying truth looks like in practical terms.

 Play It Out

It can help to play out our worries. For example, lots of people stress over family gatherings. They want everything to go
perfectly, everyone to get along, etc. But what if it doesn't go
perfectly? What if someone gets mad and stomps out the
door? Would that be the end of the world? No. It wouldn't.
It would be painful, but you would work through it. Same
with any other worry coming to pass. Would losing a job be
hard? Would a car accident be stressful? Yes. But by taking
certain steps, you would survive. Sometimes we forget the
truth of how strong we are, how good God is, how hard
times can actually bring good results. So if we can process
through the fear to imagine the potential outcome, the worry
won't consume us—we know, somehow, someway, we will
make it through—and be stronger on the other side.

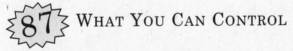 What You Can Control

The truth is, I cannot control the economy. I can't control
my adult children. I have no way of stemming natural disas-
ters or fixing a broken world. What I can control is how I re-
spond to the economy, my kids, and the next big lightning

storm. I've often repeated this phrase: "All I can do is what I can do." I know. Profound. But for me it is key. I can't fix my children, but I can love them through their journey. I can't make a dent in the national debt, but I can make sure I'm not spending more than my means. There's no way to dodge lightning, but I can make sure I'm not out there dancing with a lightning rod. If I focus on what I can control, then I am productive—I can take steps forward. If I focus on what I can't control, I end up frustrated, irritated, and crabby.

88 ONE STEP AT A TIME (YOU CAN DO THIS)

One step, one day, one breath at a time—it is the key to tackling any overwhelming circumstance in our world. I know, I'm with you—it's a truth that sounds good but is very difficult to live out. Scripture affirms it though, reminding us not to worry about tomorrow because today has enough worries of its own (see Matthew 6:34).

When you feel worry overwhelms you, when you wonder if you can take one more step, stop. Take a deep breath. Do what you can do with this day. There's tremendous freedom in embracing the hours that lie ahead, giving your best to this moment, and by will, pushing aside the rest of your concern.

89 CALL OUT IN PRAYER

God gives us a solution to our worries. He tells us to bring our burdens to him, set them at his feet, and trust he will take care of us. He encourages us to call out to him, to express gratitude for his care, and to walk away lighter (see Philippians 4:6). Sometimes we clean up our prayers, saying only what we think God wants to hear. The reality is, when we are authentic with God, he is able to touch those worried, anxious places and bring a peace only he can bring. There's no formula for heartfelt prayer; it's simply earnest conversation with the only One who is truly able to change things. Many of us hide from God when we are worried or afraid. Run to him. Pour it out. He promises he will meet you.

90 GOD IS BIGGER

God is bigger than anything we face. No matter what circumstance looms in the near future, he is bigger. So how can we allow that truth to calm our stress? alleviate our worries?

It may help to write down or memorize a few of these realities: "When you pass through the waters, I will be with you; and when you pass through the rivers, they will not sweep over you" (Isaiah 43:2). Or "The one who is in you is greater than the one who is in the world" (1 John 4:4). Memorize God's truth and then cling to it when you feel stress pouring over you. Hold tight. Repeat the words. Let them settle into the core of your heart.

91 GOD AS COMFORT

God is bigger than our circumstances, but that doesn't mean he doesn't understand and long to comfort our pain. We're not sinning if we can't see the light at the end of the tunnel or if we are heavy-hearted with concern. He is the answer to our worries, but he also has a deep understanding for the emotion that comes as we face an uncertain future. That is why over and over in the Bible, he talks of being our comfort:

I, even I, am he who comforts you. (Isaiah 51:12)

Come to me, all who are weary and burdened, and I will give you rest. (Matthew 11:28)

For just as the sufferings of Christ flow over into our
lives, so also through Christ our comfort overflows.
(2 Corinthians 1:5)

He's right here with us. He wipes our tears, he comforts
the brokenhearted (see Psalm 34:18). Sometimes one of the
sweetest truths we can embrace is that we do not walk alone.
God is with us. God is with you. Lean on him.

92 REJOICE IN SUFFERING

Scripture often talks of how we should join Jesus in his suffering. If you're anything like me, you wonder why that's really necessary. Do we have to join him in his suffering? Why?
Why does life have to be so painful? Can't we just experience
peaceful lives, grow through positive blessings, and live hap-
pily ever after?

Well, no. For a few different reasons. First, we are living
in a broken world, and not one of us escapes the heartache
that comes with that. Also, it is often in the hardest places
of life that we feel most connected to God. We discover how
desperately we need him; we call out and he meets us in
powerful ways. And finally, he will change us as we walk

through pain. If we give him access to our hearts when we're hurting, we will become more compassionate, more tender, more authentic in our faith and in our love for others.

And somehow it helps to know Jesus suffered too—that the path we walk has been walked before by our loving Savior.

93 BANISH HOPELESSNESS

Half full or half empty? Most of the time, I look at my world as the glass half full. I can typically see the good, and I know that, ultimately, God will win out. But there are moments when hopelessness invades. Everywhere I look, I feel pain. Finances are tight. Health is fragile. Relationships fail. Friends betray. God is distant.

In moments like that, I desperately need to be intentional about capturing my thoughts—"Hope deferred makes the heart sick" (Proverbs 13:12)—while 2 Corinthians 10:5 instructs us to take every thought captive. I can't stay too long in the dark place of hopelessness. I have to intentionally embrace truth, hold on to God's promises and banish hopelessness. I force myself to view the glass half full, sometimes by will alone.

94 Beware of Liars in Truth-Teller Clothing

There's nothing that will add to your stress more than someone who touts truth but lives a lie. If you have a friend who sees nothing but the bad, who focuses on everything going wrong, chances are you will start looking through the same lens. And here's the truth—that individual may call herself a realist or a truth teller, but you know in your heart that highlighting every potential harm is not truth telling; it's complaining. While you want to be there for friends who are hurting, you want to distance yourself from people who weigh you down with an endless series of negative opinions.

95 Good Will Come

It seems impossible. What good can come from *this*? I've said that more times than I can count. Typically though, I'll see it over time. I was divorced in my early twenties and spent twelve years alone as a single parent. I remember the anger I felt over my circumstances—what good can come from *this*? And yet, today, I have the sweet privilege of reaching out and walking alongside young single moms. I know where they are because I've been there. Being with them gives me such joy—greater than I ever would have expected. That joy is a direct result of the hardship I went through. I've seen good come from many of the painful things I've walked through, enough so that I trust it more now. Not that I always understand or see the good (and I may not while I'm on this earth), but I do, by will, know that God will use the yuck in my world to bring about treasure. That kind of knowledge helps ease the pain of the moment.

96 IT DOES END

When believing that good will come isn't quite enough, it may help to know one basic truth: it will end. Whatever we are facing will come to an end. It may be a month or a season, but ultimately, we will close the door on this stress or hardship. Maybe you can't sell your home, maybe you're out of a job, it could be you are facing a physical illness or a painful relational connection. Whatever you are dealing with right now will look very different in just a few days, months, or even years. Things I thought I would never live through are now distant memories. Fears that consumed me ten years ago no longer linger in my heart. When all else fails, it can be good to remember that age-old truth: "This too shall pass."

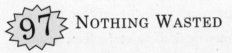 97 NOTHING WASTED

Sometimes I worry that what I'm doing, giving, working toward will be for naught. What if my love isn't received? What if my hard work goes unnoticed? Or on a much larger scale, as we look ahead to our son's kidney transplant: what if my husband gives his kidney to our son, and something goes terribly wrong? I know I'm not alone. We've all had moments where we wonder if anything we do really matters. If the outcome isn't what we expect, was it worth it in the first place? And this is where we have to remind ourselves of the truth: no love, no effort, no selfless act is ever wasted. Granted, it may not have the desired outcome, but selfless love, hard work, kindness extended will make a difference—either in our lives, in the lives of the recipients, or in the lives of those watching. No good thing is wasted.

Knowing that can give us the strength to continue on when we feel discouraged.

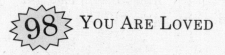 ## 98 YOU ARE LOVED

I'm no spring chick anymore. I'm not old, but I'm not young. And I still call my mommy. It's true. When I'm worried, happy, fearful, angry, or celebratory, I call my mom. I know that she loves me. I know that she cares. She typically can't fix the problem I am facing; yet it doesn't seem to matter. Just knowing that her heart aches with mine, that her smile stretches with my own…makes me feel better. So it is with God. He loves you. He loves you as you chew on your nails or furrow your brow. He loves you as you process through the fifty different ways that things could go wrong. He loves your smile. He wipes your tears. He doesn't love the cleaned-up version of who you are. He loves the messy, slightly neurotic, often humbled reality of you. When we know that, when we run to that kind of all-encompassing love, there is nothing we can't face. Even if a problem remains unchanged, being able to rest in that kind of love makes all the difference in how we face it.

 HEAVEN

This is not our home. This broken, mangled, hurting planet is not where we'll land when all is said and done. God has a better place, and he calls us to remember it. Matthew 5:12 reminds us not to let the betrayals of this world steal our hope: "Rejoice and be glad, because great is your reward in heaven." When we run into resistance, when we experience heartache, we can know that God will make things right, he will wipe every tear. And as we remain faithful through all the pain, we hold on to 2 Corinthians 4:16–18: "Therefore we do not lose heart. Though outwardly we are wasting away, yet inwardly we are being renewed day by day. For our light and momentary troubles are achieving for us an eternal glory that far outweighs them all. So we fix our eyes not on what is seen, but on what is unseen. For what is seen is temporary, but what is unseen is eternal."

We have no idea what God has in store for us. Like a loving parent on Christmas Eve, he is excited to unveil our new home. "No eye has seen, no ear has heard, no mind has conceived what God has prepared for those who love him" (1 Corinthians 2:9).

SUMMARY

Don't give up, friend. Don't give in. Use the tools presented in this book to help see you through this season of life. And always keep in mind that this is your temporary home. If you have said yes to the gift of life that Jesus offers, you will one day pass out of this place and into his world, where all will be made right—where our Savior will look at you with gentle eyes and say with pride, "Well done, good and faithful servant, well done."

More 99 Ways for
only $5.99!

99 Ways
to Increase
Your Income

Frank Martin

99 Ways
to Stretch Your
Home Budget

Cheri Gillard

99 Ways
to Fight Worry
and Stress

Elsa Kok Colopy

99 Ways
to Entertain Your
Family for Free

Mack Thomas

99 Ways
to Build
Job Security

Gary Nowinski

99 Bible
Promises for
Tough Times

Randy Petersen

In challenging times we all need advice on how to overcome stress and find encouragement. The 99 Ways books offer up-to-date, practical, and reliable information in a succinct format at a price anyone can afford.